A Kid's Guide to Black Holes Astronomy Books Grade 6

Astronomy & Space Science

BABY PROFESSOR

EDUCATION KIDS

Speedy Publishing LLC
40 E. Main St. #1156
Newark, DE 19711
www.speedypublishing.com
Copyright 2016

Have you ever watched the sky at
night and wondered if there are
other things, aside from the stars and
the moon, that exist out there,
beyond planet Earth?
Do black holes really exist?
Have you heard of the
Big Bang Theory?

The best way to understand all of it is to study astronomy. What is astronomy? It is simply the study of the solar system, the universe, and different phenomena in space.

Do you know what the Solar System consists of?

The sun, planets,
moon, stars, asteroids,
comets, gas, and dust
are what our Solar
System is made up of.
Through astronomy,
we know the scientific
explanations of
the formation of
the solar system.

All that exists in the Solar System revolves around the Sun. It is found in the center of the Solar System. Because of the Sun's powerful gravity, it draws the other objects in the Solar System toward it. All the objects are moving quickly, so if the Sun had no gravity, the objects, including our earth, would just fly off in all directions.

Can you name all
the planets in our
Solar System?

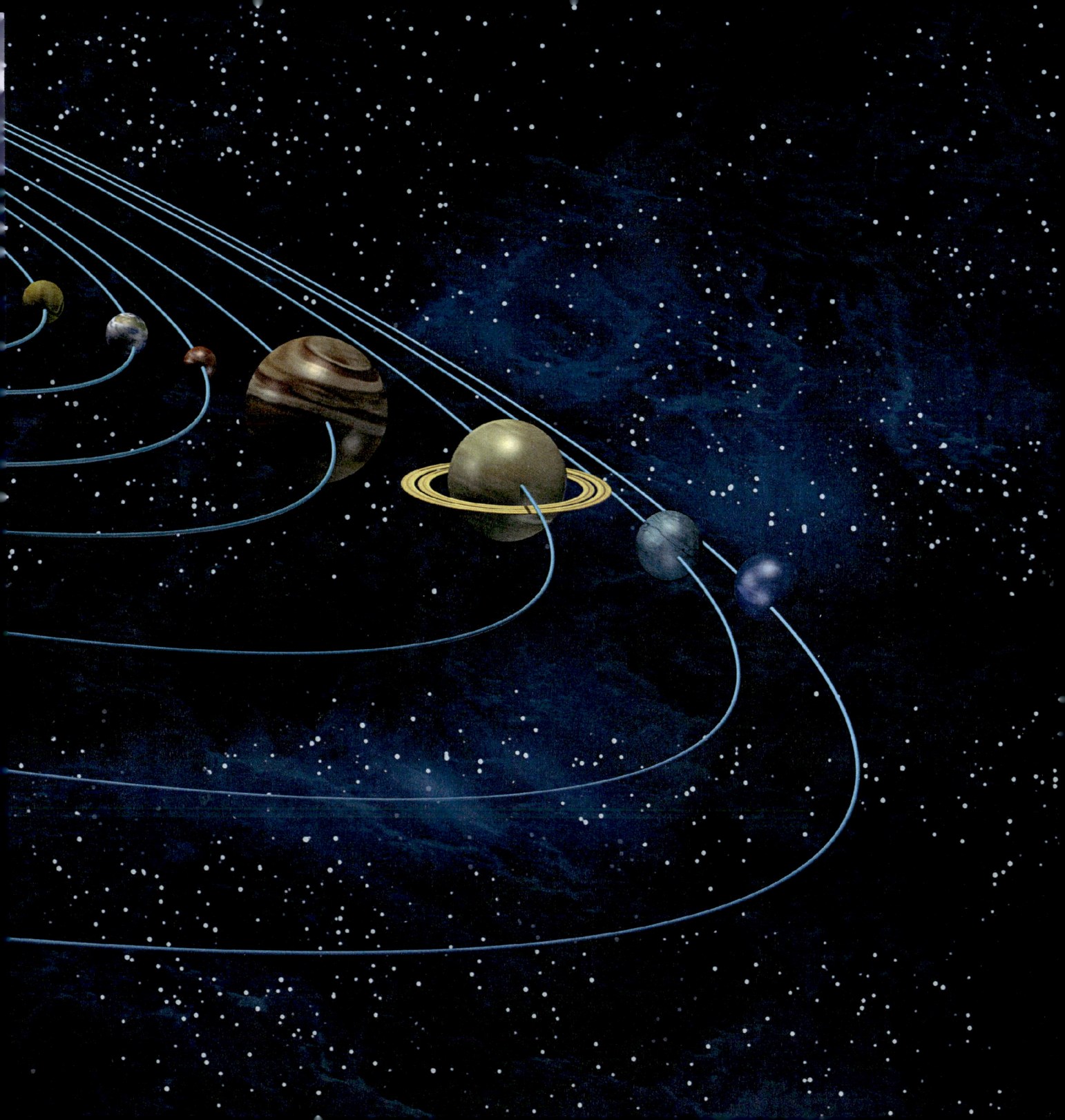

There are eight
planets in the
Solar System:

Mercury - the closest
planet from the sun
and the smallest
among all planets

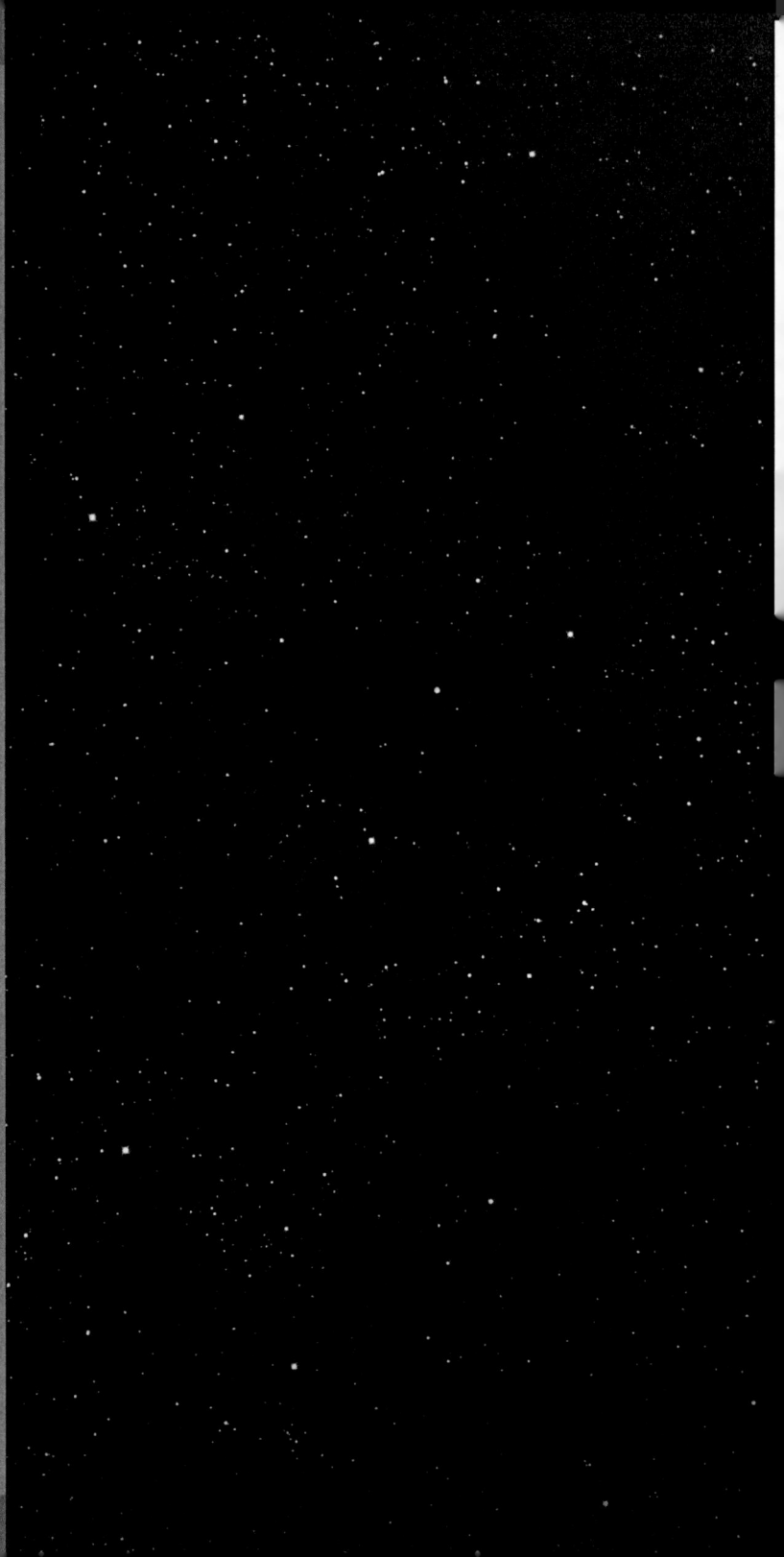

Venus - the
brightest planet
we can see and
the second planet
from the Sun

Earth - the fifth
largest planet in
the Solar System
and the third planet
from the Sun. It only
has one moon.

Mars - the fourth planet from the Sun and the second smallest planet, next to Mercury. It has two moons.

Jupiter - the largest
planet in the Solar
System and the fifth
planet from the Sun. It
has at least 67 moons.

Saturn - the second largest planet and sixth planet from the Sun. It has 53 confirmed and named moons

Uranus - has a band of 13 rings and is the seventh planet from the Sun. It has at least 21 moons.

Neptune - the eighth planet from the Sun, with 14 moons.

Pluto used to be called the ninth planet, but it does not satisfy certain parts of what defines a planet, so it has been demoted. But it is still part of the Solar System!

Do you know what caused the formation of the Universe?

Billions of years ago, astronomers believe, an explosion caused the formation of the Universe. This theory is known as the Big Bang Theory. The explosion produced all matter and all energy.

The Big Bang theory tries to explain how the stars, planets, and everything in space exist.

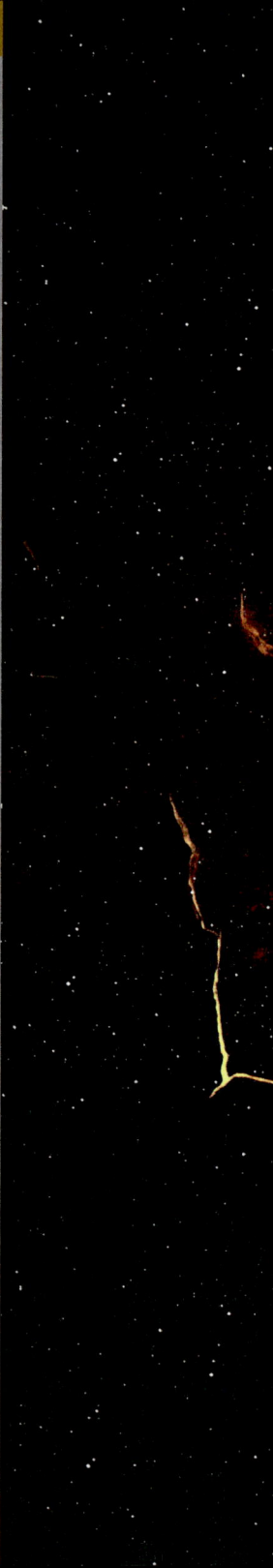

Is there really a

black hole?

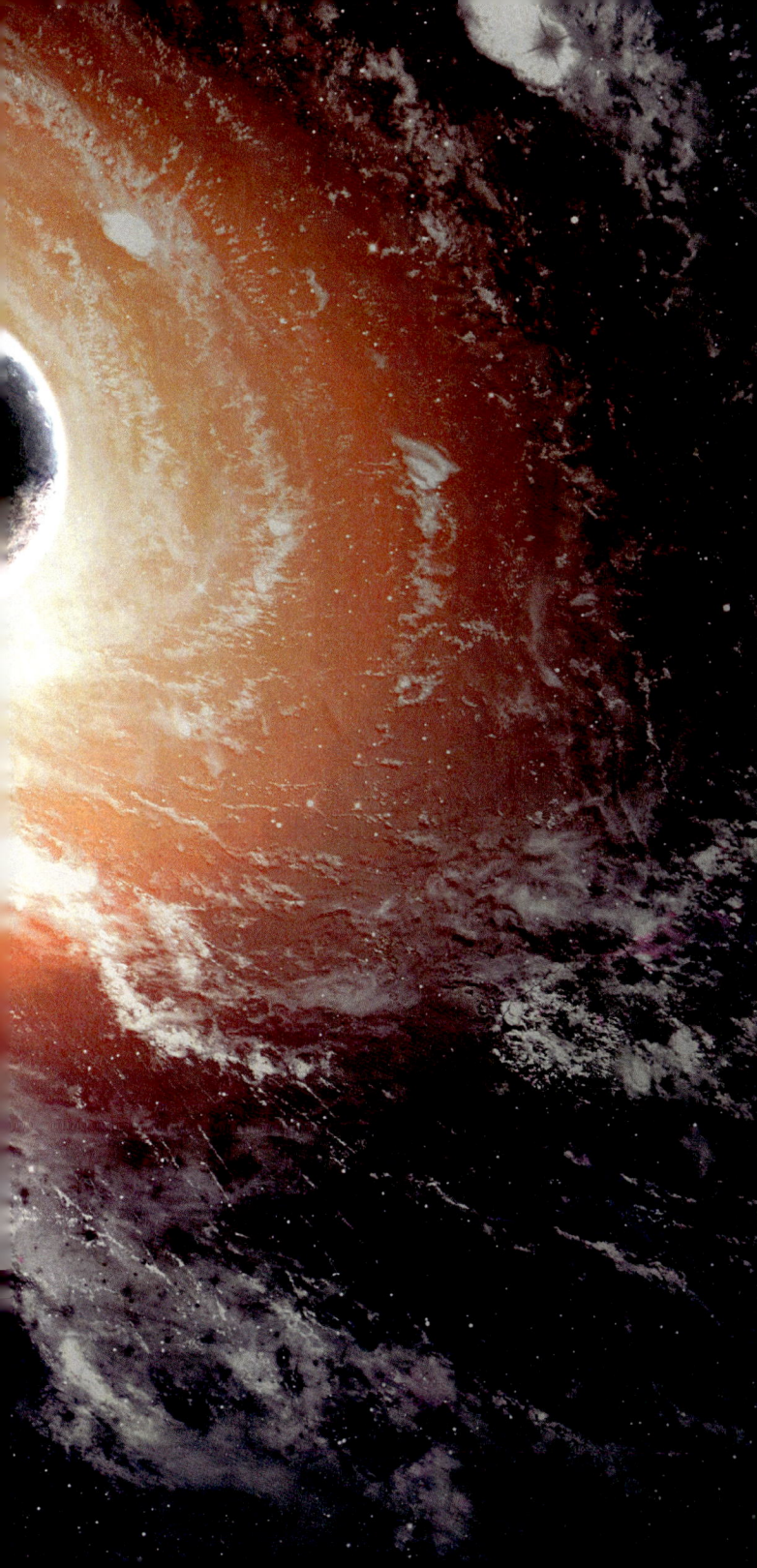

According to astronomers, black holes can be found in the universe. A black hole is quite strange because it doesn't have a surface but it has a very powerful gravity that pulls anything towards it, including light.

You can imagine
what a black hole is
when you try using
a vacuum cleaner.
Once you turn on the
vacuum, you will see
that all the dirt and
dust are sucked by
the vacuum cleaner.

The vacuum cleaner uses suction to get everything inside the vacuum cleaner while a black hole uses gravity to pull objects towards it.

How big do you think
asteroids are?

Where can we
find them?

Asteroids can be found in the "Asteroid Belt". There are more than 200 asteroids that can be found in the asteroid belt, between the orbits of Mars and Jupiter. Asteroids are rocky, airless objects that revolve around the Sun.

Asteroids differ in size from each other. The smallest discovered asteroid was about 20 feet across. At the other extreme is the dwarf planet "Ceres" which has a diameter of approximately 945 kilometers.

A Comet, on the other hand, is a small icy body of rock made of frozen gases and dust. These objects can be found in the Kuiper Belt which is beyond the orbit of the dwarf planet Pluto, but we see them in the night sky when their orbits bring them close to the Sun. They are mostly sphere-shaped.

A comet's size really depends on how close it is to the Sun. As it goes closer to the Sun, it heats up and forms a cloud called a coma. It leaves debris behind which causes meteor showers that can be visible on Earth.

Comets also have tails. A small comet can be as big as a house and a big comet can be as big as a small town.

The most famous
comets so far
discovered are
Halley's Comet and
Encke's Comet.

Knowing the
evolution of the
universe enables us to
appreciate astronomy.
There are many things
in space that we
don't understand yet
but through studying
astronomy we will
get to understand
each phenomenon
little by little.

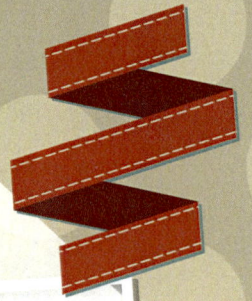

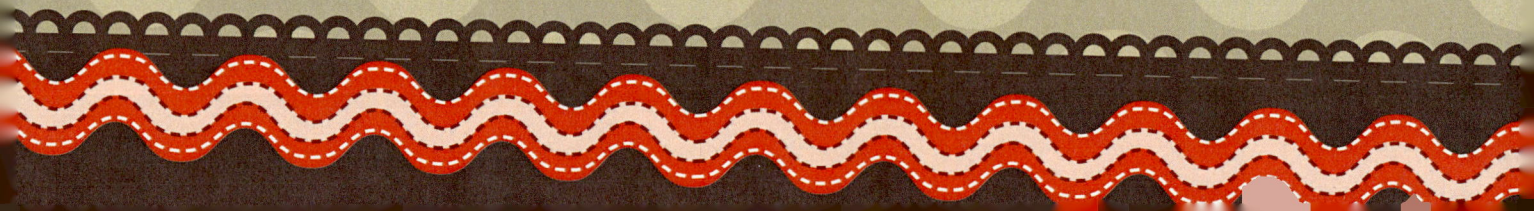

Visit

BABY PROFESSOR
EDUCATION KIDS

www.BabyProfessorBooks.com

to download Free Baby Professor eBooks
and view our catalog of new and exciting
Children's Books

Made in the USA
San Bernardino, CA
03 October 2018